B Flat Clarinet/Bass Clarinet

Book One
Beginning

T0057347

THE BAND METHOD THAT TEACHES MUSIC READING

RHYTHM
MASTER

Supplemental Material

By

J.R. McEntyre
Coordinator of Music, Retired
Odessa Public Schools
Odessa, Texas

And

Harry H. Haines
Music Department Chairman
West Texas State University
Canyon, Texas

Clarinet Fingering Chart

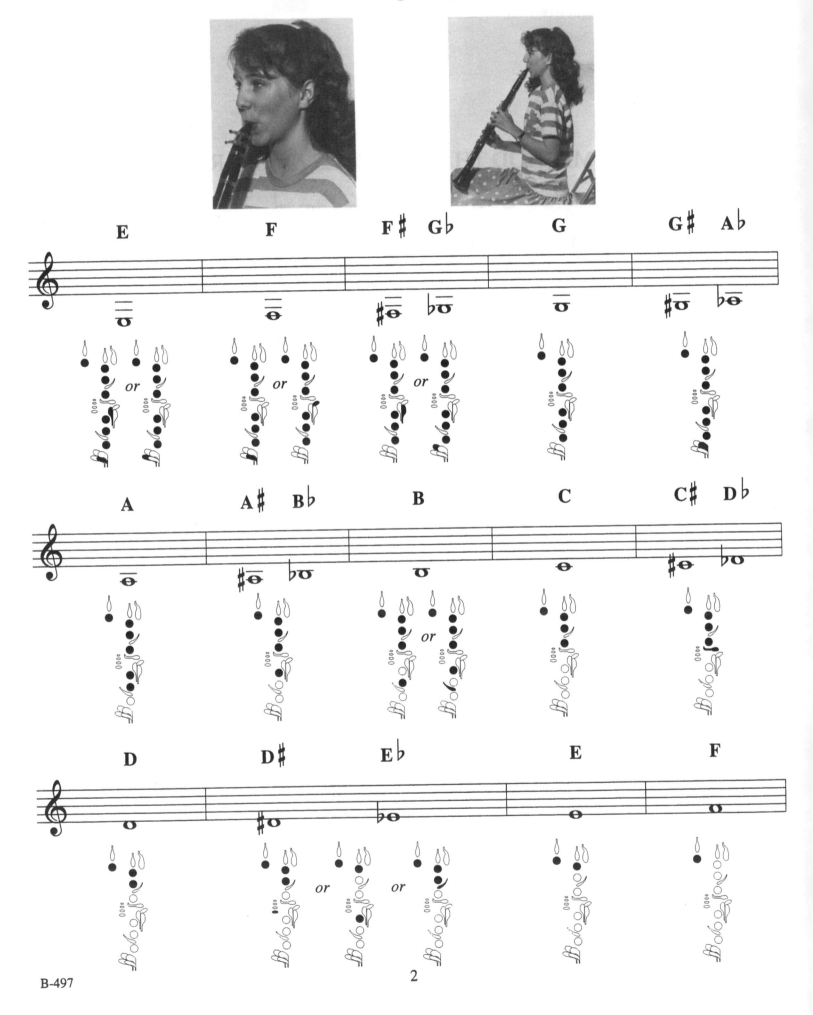

2

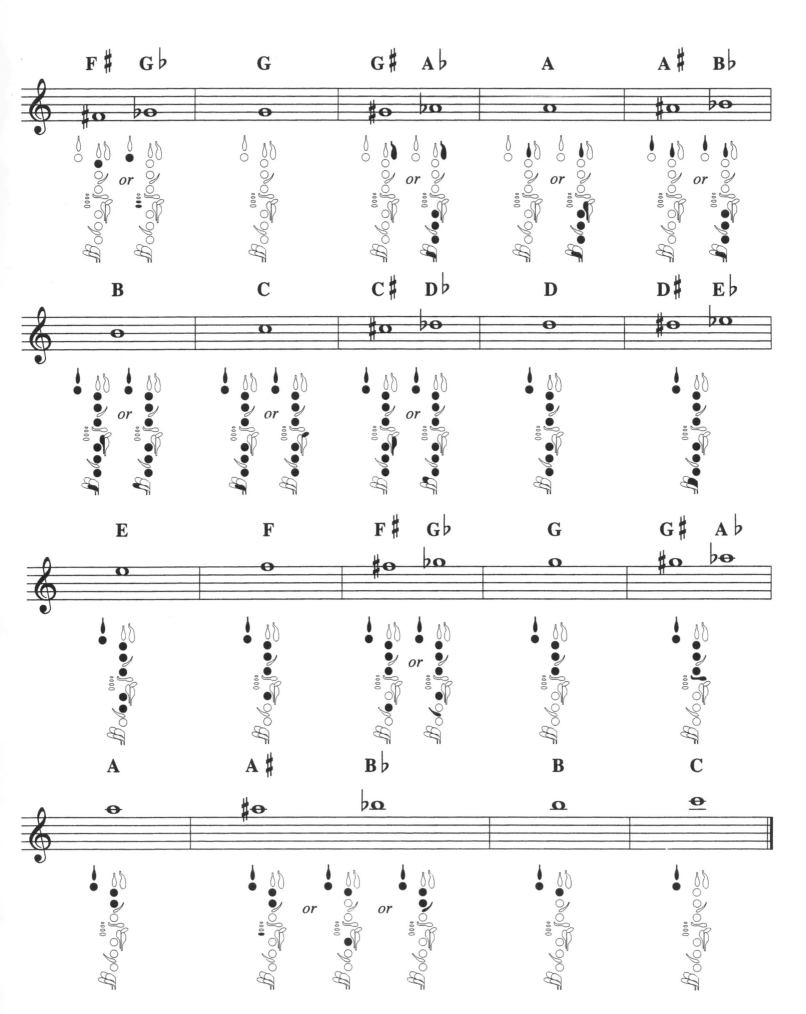

Preliminary Lesson
The Most Important Lesson!

Some aspects of learning to play a band instrument are best learned without an instruction book. This is especially true of the very first stages such as 1) putting the instrument together, 2) learning correct posture and position, and 3) producing the sound. Also, an understanding of a few basic music symbols will be a great help in beginning to read a method book. The authors believe that best results will be achieved if the teacher approaches this lesson using a Suzuki-like presentation. The basis should be rote teaching using much imitation and repetition.

The **Conductor's Guide** contains specific information about each instrument and suggestions from a master teacher for introducing the embouchure.

How long should you spend on a **Preliminary Lesson**? Teaching situations vary but most successful beginning band classes we know get better results when they spend four or five hours on this material. At a minimum, tone production and articulation should be established to a point where students are able to consistently produce the pitch for their first note in **LESSON 1**.

1 Start with the mouthpiece only. Your teacher will show you how to wet the reed and use the ligature to attach it to the mouthpiece. Add the barrel joint and work to produce a good, firm squawk. A good, firm embouchure should produce a pitch close to "F#."

2 Work on correct posture. Pay careful attention to your teacher's instructions. Air is the lifeblood of your sound. No one can play an instrument well unless he/she has good breath support. Good posture is an acquired habit and the time to start is the first day.

3 Put the instrument together properly and learn to hold it correctly. Practice this many times until you can do it well. Instruments may look strong but they are really quite delicate and are easily damaged. Each student must learn how to care for his/her instrument and there will never be a better time than now.

4 Produce a characteristic sound. To do this requires much repetition. Every person learns to play an instrument by the "trial and error" method. One of the essential aspects of success is to "try" enough times to give the method a chance for learning to occur. Repetition, correct instruction, and constant, intelligent analysis are the three primary aspects of learning to play an instrument. The most important of these is (you guessed it) _repetition_! You must go over and over your basic sound always trying to make it better.

5 Practice articulation. Start the sound with your tongue and release with your breath. Learning how to begin and end a tone and coordinate the use of your tongue should be a major goal of this **Preliminary Lesson**.

6 Finally, every student must learn a few basic music symbols before he/she can begin to read music. **LESSON 1** will be much easier if you know the musical terms below. Throughout this book, the red, numbered flags refer to the **Index of Musical Terms** found on the back cover.

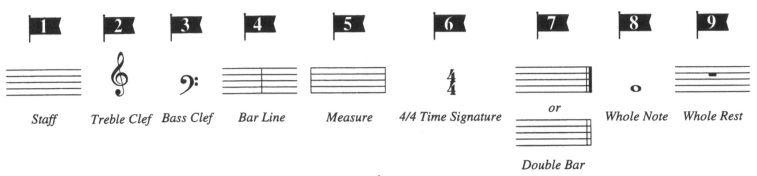

LESSON 1
The First Note

G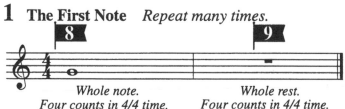

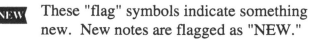
NEW — These "flag" symbols indicate something new. New notes are flagged as "NEW."

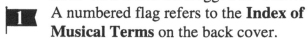
1 — A numbered flag refers to the **Index of Musical Terms** on the back cover.

1 The First Note   *Repeat many times.*

Good tone quality requires good breath support. You cannot become an outstanding player unless you have a supported sound.

Whole note.
Four counts in 4/4 time.

Whole rest.
Four counts in 4/4 time.

2 Whole Notes and Whole Rests   *Count each line carefully. Count the rests silently.*

3 Quarter Notes and Quarter Rests

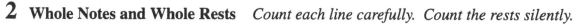

4 Mixing It Up

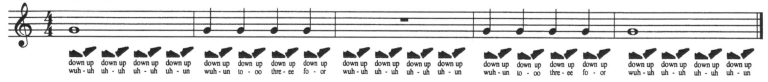

5 Half Notes and Half Rests

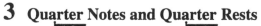

6 All Kinds of Notes

7 All Kinds of Rests   *Write the counting on the lines below the staff.*

_____   _____   _____   _____

LESSON 2
The Second Note

F

Tap your foot, count, and play every line.

8 The Second Note   *Repeat many times.*

9 Practice the New Note

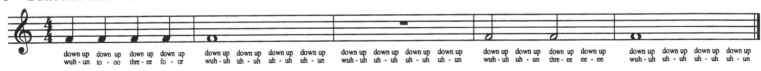

10 Two-Note Song   *Write the counting on the lines below the staff.*

11 First Duet   [14]

12 Duet Part

13 Quarter Notes and Quarter Rests

14 All Kinds of Notes

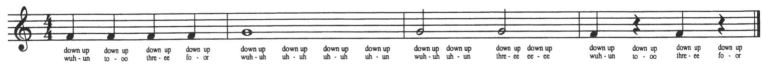

15 Who Will Play in the Rest?

SUGGESTION: Start every class using Warm-up #1 on the inside of the front cover.

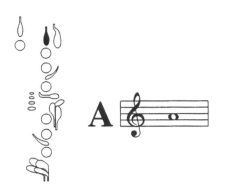

LESSON 3
Three Notes

A

Good players can read music. Remember to tap your foot, count, and play every line.

16 **The Third Note** *Repeat many times.*

17 **Three-Note Exercise**

down up | down up | down up | down up | down up | down up | down up | down up | down up | down up | down up | down up | down up | down up | down up | down up
wuh - uh | uh - un | thre - ee | ee - ee | wuh - uh | uh - un | thre - ee | ee - ee | wuh - uh | uh - un | thre - ee | ee - ee | wuh - uh | uh - un | thre - ee | ee - ee

18 **Echo Song**

solo **15** *class*   *solo*   *class*   *solo*   *class*   *solo*   *everyone*

19 **Duet: Hand Clappers**

20 **Duet: Finger Snappers**

21 **All Kinds of Notes**

22 **Who Will Play in the Rest (Again)?**

23 **Our First Song**

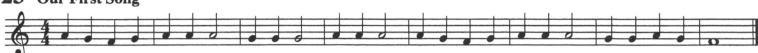

LESSON 4
The Eighth Note Lesson

Always carry your instrument case with the lid toward you.

24 Introducing Eighth Notes

down up down up down up down up   down up down up down up down up down up down up down up down up   down up down up down up down up

25 Eighth Notes and Quarter Notes   *Write the counting on the lines below the staff.*

_____   _____   _____   _____

26 Sneaky Second Count

27 Tricky Third Count

28 Freaky Fourth Count

SPECIAL ASSIGNMENT: Before going to line 29, try to count and play the first measures of 25, 26, 27, and 28 straight down the page. Then do the second measures, then the third, etc. This is a great exercise in rhythm!

29 All Mixed Up

30 Hot Cross Buns

31 Merrily We Speed Along

LESSON 5
The Fourth Note/Dotted Half Note Lesson

E

A dot after a note adds one half the value of that note.

32 **New-Note Exercise**

33 **Introducing the Dotted Half Note**   *Write the counting on the lines below the staff.*

34 **Low Note-High Note**

35 **Etude for Clarinet**   *Roll the first finger, clarinets!*

36 **Echo Song #2**

solo   class   solo   class   solo   class   solo   all

37 **Go Tell Aunt Rhodie**   *Right hand down on all the half note A's.*

38 **Yankee's First Half**   *The entire song is in Lesson 15.*

39 **Paris Duet**

40 **Duet Part**   *harmony*

accompaniment

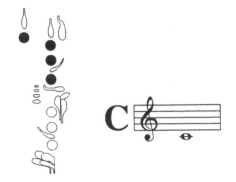

LESSON 6
The 2/4 Lesson

C

D

41 **The Most Famous Note** *Repeat many times.*

NEW

42 **Trumpet "Kick" Note** *Repeat many times.*

NEW

43 **Back and Forth**

44 **Solo Line**

45 **Class Line**

46 **Introducing 2/4 Time**

20

47 **Grand Ole Duke of York** *The hardest line in the book so far!*

48 **Twinkle Twinkle** *Ask your director why there is no double bar here!*

SUGGESTION: Expand your warm-up to include Warm-up #2 (and play it from memory).

Rhythm Set #1
Eighth, Quarter, Half, and Whole Note Rhythms

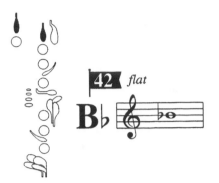

LESSON 7
The 3/4 Lesson

42 *flat*

B♭

Right hand down on all throat tones when playing long notes.

49 High Note *Write the counting on the lines below the staff.*

21 **NEW**

How many counts?

50 Building Range *Go back to the beginning of this line.* **24**

Right Hand Down   *R.H. Down*

51 Eighth Note Etude **24** *Go back to the first repeat sign.*

R.H. Down - - - - - -

52 Variations on Line 51

53 Duet: Hand Clappers

54 Duet: Knee Slappers

55 Blow the Man Down

56 Hymn Tune

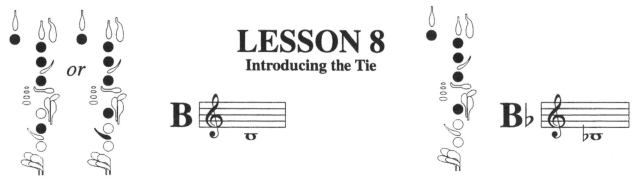

LESSON 8
Introducing the Tie

57 **Low B Natural** *Repeat many times.* NEW 25

58 **Low B Flat** *Repeat many times.* NEW

59 **Two New Notes** 44 *natural*

60 **Chromatic Woodwinds and High Brass**

Ask your director when to use the alternate fingering.

61 **Some Folks Do**

62 **First and Second Endings** 26

1.

2.

Pop!

63 **Mary in a New Key**

64 **This Old Man**

65 **Long-Note Challenge** *How long can you hold this note? Sneak a breath if you have to.*

66 **Brother John** 27 *round*

1

2

3

4

LESSON 9
The Dotted Quarter Lesson

Learn how to clean and care
for your instrument properly.

67 **Introducing the Dotted Quarter and Eighth Rest**

Eighth notes are sometimes written with a single flag on the stem.

68 **Another Way (To Introduce the Dotted Quarter and Eighth Rest)**

69 **Dotted Quarters Everywhere**

70 **Song with Dotted Quarter**

71 **America**

72 **Alma Mater**

73 **Careless Love**

SUGGESTION: Add the first two measures of Warm-up #3 to your daily routine.

Rhythm Set #2
Dotted Quarter Rhythms

LESSON 10
Dotted Quarter Drill

You can tell how good players are by the way they look. Good players have good posture and instrument position.

74 **A Lower Note**

75 **Low-Note Drill**

76 **Dotted Quarter Drill**

77 **Hand Clappers**

78 **Knee Slappers**

79 **Goin' Home**

80 **All through the Night**

81 **Crazy Rhythm Bridge**

82 **Duet Part**

LESSON 11
The Slur Lesson

83 Slurring Smoothly

Many people confuse a slur and a tie. How are they different?

84 Dedicated to Clarinets

85 Dedicated to Everyone Else

86 High and Low Notes

87 French Song (with Pick-up Notes)

How do you count the first two notes?

88 Sweetly Sings the Donkey (Round)

89 Aura Lee

Congratulations! You're half-way through the book!

LESSON 12
Building the Chalameau

Are you playing with good hand position?

90 Clarinet Teeth-Rattler
91 F Scale
92 F Scale Drill
93 Hymn Tune in 2/4 Time
94 Jingle Bells
95 Jolly Ole St. Nick
96 Finger Snappers
97 Hand Clappers

Clarinets Only

Supplementary Lesson

Look up any unfamiliar notes in the
Fingering Chart *on pages 2 and 3.*

A **Introducing the High Register**

B **Going Higher**

C **Higher Still**

D **Slurring to High Notes**

E **Four New High Notes**

F **All High Register**

G **Familiar Fingerings**

H **Dear, Dear, What Can the Matter Be?**

LESSON 13
Clarinet High Register

To make a good slur, keep the breath flowing.

98 "The" Scale

99 Clarinets' Line

100 Clarinets Higher

101 Clarinets Higher Still

102 Barcarolle

103 Barcarolle Again *Dedicated to clarinets.*

104 One More Song

SUGGESTION: Gradually add all of Warm-up #3 to your daily routine.

LESSON 14
Introducing Dynamics

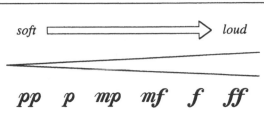

*To get a good tone you
must blow very fast air.*

105 **Loud Etude**

106 **Soft Exercise** *Does this sound familiar?*

107 **Swing Low**

108 **Mexican Song**

109 **Duet: Part One**

110 **Duet: Part Two**

111 **Clarinets Can't Play This Now - Maybe Later?**

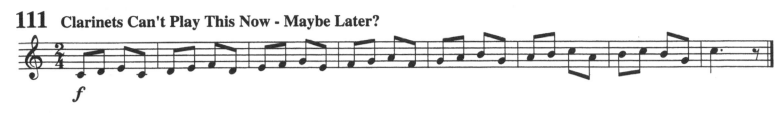

LESSON 15
The Key Signature Lesson

A note "out of key" is a wrong note.

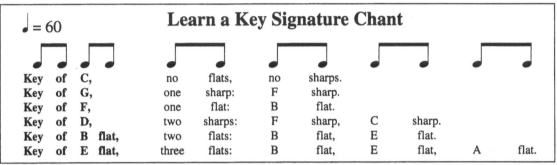

Learn a Key Signature Chant

♩ = 60

Key	of	C,	no	flats,	no	sharps.		
Key	of	G,	one	sharp:	F	sharp.		
Key	of	F,	one	flat:	B	flat.		
Key	of	D,	two	sharps:	F	sharp,	C	sharp.
Key	of	B flat,	two	flats:	B	flat,	E	flat.
Key	of	E flat,	three	flats:	B	flat,	E	flat,	A	flat.

Later, your director will perhaps give you a specific chant for each line.

112 Yankee Doodle with Key Signature

113 Same Song, Different Key

114 Mary Ann

115 Etude in Three Keys

Key of F, one flat: B flat.   *Key of C, no flats, no sharps.*   *Key of G, one sharp: F sharp.*

LESSON 16
The Cut-Time Lesson

A great deal of music is written in cut-time. Composers like it because it is less work to write.

116 **Scale in Cut-Time**

117 **Cut-Time Compared**

118 **Same Line, Different Time**

119 **Good King Wenceslas**

120 **Michael, Row the Boat Ashore**

121 **Lightly Row**

122 **Marine's Hymn**

LESSON 17
Introducing Afterbeats

123 **Variations on "Sol-La-Ti-Do"**

Variation 1

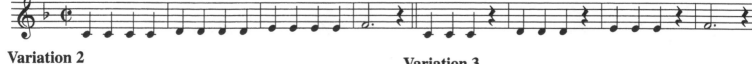

Variation 2

Variation 3

Variation 4

Variation 5

124 **Oom-Pa**

23 *afterbeat*

125 **Duet Part**

126 **John Jacob Jingle**

Solo

f

"Pa"

mp

"Oom"

mp

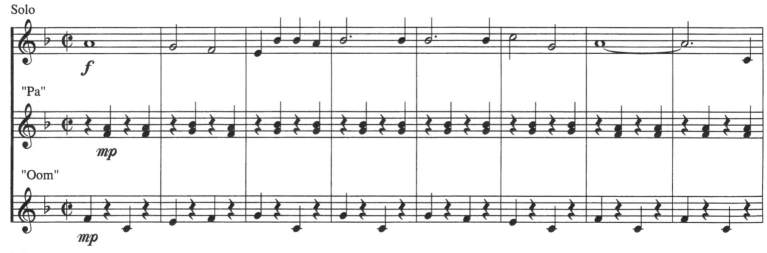

Solo

"Pa"

"Oom"

LESSON 18
Syncopation

Always play up-beat notes exactly on the up-beat, not early.

127 **Syncopation**

128 **Syncopation Exercise**

129 **Our Boys Will Shine (Shortened Version)**

130 **Camptown Races** *Where are the syncopated notes?*

131 **Mixed-Up McDonald**

132 **Tom Dooley**

133 **Accompaniment**

LESSON 19
Building Rhythmic Independence

134 Counting Syncopation

135 Syncopation in Cut-Time

136 Good Night, Ladies

137 Dem Bones

138 March for Hand-Clappers, Knee-Slappers, Finger-Snappers, and Foot-Stompers

A. Hand-Clappers

B. Knee-Slappers

C. Finger-Snappers

D. Foot-Stompers

A.

B.

C.

D.

Optional Supplementary Rhythm Set
Sixteenth Notes

3/8 and 6/8 (Compound) Time

Optional Supplementary Lesson #1
Sixteenth Notes

A **Scale with Sixteenth Notes**

B **Bird**

C **Polly Wolly Doodle**

D **Ring-a-Ding-a-Ding**

E **Scale with Two Sixteenths**

F **Skip to My Lou**

Optional Supplementary Lesson #2
6/8 and 3/8 Time

Special Songs for Individual Practice

Look up any unfamiliar notes in the
Fingering Chart *on pages 2 and 3.*

Up on the Housetop

America the Beautiful

Red River Valley

Taps

Reveille

Special Songs for Individual Practice

Look up any unfamiliar notes in the
Fingering Chart *on pages 2 and 3.*

Reuben and Rachel

Eency Weency Spider

Scales to Prepare for Book Two

F Concert Major Scale

E Flat Concert Major Scale

B Flat Concert Major Scale

B Flat Concert Chromatic Scale

Traditional "One And" Counting System*

Most teachers of band instruments agree that the teaching of music reading can be done most efficiently and effectively with a counting system. A rhythmic vocabulary helps communication and promotes understanding. It doesn't seem to matter which counting system is used as long as there is a system and it is used consistently. Two suggested counting systems are offered on these two pages.

The idea of saying the "number" of the count on which a note occurs and saying the word, "and," for any note that occurs half-way after the beat has been used for many years. The basic idea with many variations can be found in hundreds of music books. Probably the most widely circulated publication using this system of counting is the *Haskell Harr Drum Method*. Because of its long history (published in 1937 and still used today), its expansive use, and the general public perception that percussionists are supposedly experts at counting, many band directors have adapted a counting system that is remarkably similar. The following is a somewhat modified summary of "one and" counting that might be used by teachers and students for this band method:

I. Notes of One or More Counts

For notes of one count (or longer), simply say the number of the count on which the note begins and continue counting for the duration of the note. Thus, a note which receives one count and which begins on the first beat of the measure would be counted, "one." If the note occurs on the second count say, "two," etc. A note of longer value would simply be counted longer. The following example quickly illustrates the counting system as applied to rhythms (including rests) of one, two, three, or four counts:

II. Counting the Sub-divisions

Notes which receive less than a whole count and which are divisible by two (some would say simple time) are counted as follows:

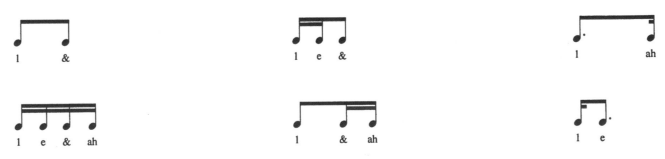

Notes which receive less than a whole count and which are divisible by three (some would say compound time) are counted as follows:

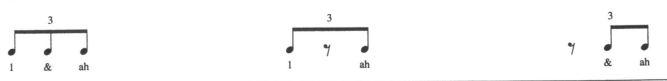

---

*For a complete explanation of this counting system, see *the Haskell Harr Drum Method*, published by M. M. Cole Publishing Company.

Eastman Counting System*

there is no "official" counting system endorsed by the Eastman School of Music, there was a system written by Alan I. McHose which was published in his series of theory texts. Because he was a theory instructor at the Eastman School for many years and his books were used as textbooks for his theory classes, most Eastman students of the 1940s, 50s, and 60s used his counting syllables.

For almost a third of a century these graduates of one of America's largest and most highly regarded music schools have been doing a great deal of "evangelizing" about their counting system. Many have been leaders in music education and their teaching techniques have been widely copied. The authors of this band method, neither of whom attended the Eastman School, have adapted the system and used a modified version in teaching beginning band classes. Both recommend its use with this band method.

I. Notes of One or More Counts

Notes of one count (or longer) are counted much the same way as in any other counting system. One major difference is that notes longer than one count are held with a continuous word-sound. Thus, a whole note in 4/4 time would be counted, "onnnnnnnnne," for four counts. The following example quickly illustrates the counting system as applied to rhythms (including rests) of one, two, three, or four counts:

II. Counting the Sub-divisions

Notes which receive less than a whole count are categorized into rhythms which are divisible by two or those which are divisible by three (some would say duple and triple rhythms). Again, any note which occurs on a downbeat is simply counted with the number of the count. The important difference is that a note which occurs on the last half of a count is counted, "te," (Latin, rhymes with May) and notes which occur on the second or third fraction of the count are counted; "lah," and, "lee." Everything else is counted, "ta" (pronounced, "tah").

Rhythms Which are Divisible by Two (Read Down)   Rhythms Which are Divisible by Three (Read Down)

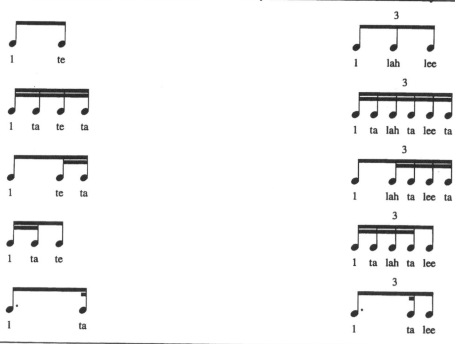

*For a complete explanation of this counting system, see the *Ear Training and Sight Singing Dictation Manual*, published by Prentice Hall.

Warm-ups

Play a good, strong tone.

*Look up any unfamiliar notes in the **Fingering Chart** on pages 2 and 3.*

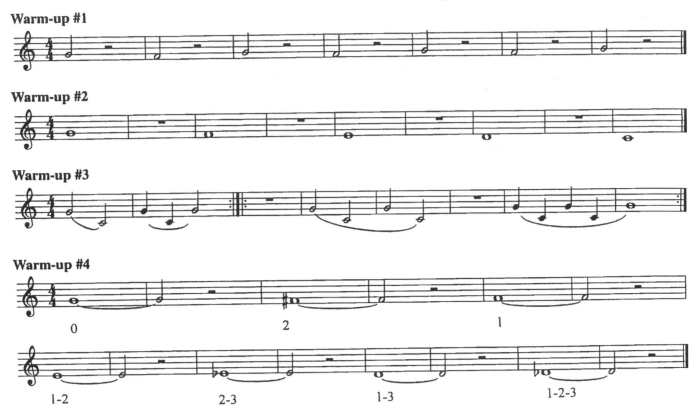

Practice Record Chart

Week	Day 1	Day 2	Day 3	Day 4	Day 5	Day 6	Day 7	Total Time	Parent's Initials	Weekly Grade	Week	Day 1	Day 2	Day 3	Day 4	Day 5	Day 6	Day 7	Total Time	Parent's Initials	Weekly Grade
1											19										
2											20										
3											21										
4											22										
5											23										
6											24										
7											25										
8											26										
9											27										
10											28										
11											29										
12											30										
13											31										
14											32										
15											33										
16											34										
17											35										
18											36										

Index of Musical Terms

1 **Staff -** the five lines and four spaces where notes are placed

2 **Treble Clef -** a symbol that indicates which notes are on each line and space of the staff; also called the "G" clef

3 **Bass Clef -** a symbol that indicates which notes are on each line and space of the staff; also called the "F" clef

4 **Bar Line -** divides the staff into measures

5 **Measure -** the space between two bar lines

6 **4/4 Time Signature -** The numeral on top indicates that there are four beats in each measure. The bottom numeral indicates that each quarter note gets one beat.

7 **Double Bar -** marks the end of a section

8 **Whole Note -** gets four beats in any time signature with a 4 as the bottom numeral, such as 4/4 time; equivalent to two half notes

9 **Whole Rest -** gets four beats in any time signature with a 4 as the bottom numeral (except 3/4); equivalent to two half rests

10 **Quarter Note -** gets one beat in any time signature with a 4 as the bottom numeral; equivalent to two eighth notes

11 **Quarter Rest -** gets one beat in any time signature with a 4 as the bottom numeral; equivalent to two eighth rests

12 **Half Note -** gets two beats in any time signature with a 4 as the bottom numeral; equivalent to two quarter notes

13 **Half Rest -** gets two beats in any time signature with a 4 as the bottom numeral; equivalent to two quarter rests

14 **Duet -** a song for two players or two parts

15 **Solo -** means that the part is to be played by one person

16 **Eighth Note -** gets half a beat in any time signature with a 4 as the bottom numeral; equivalent to two sixteenth notes

17 **Dotted Half Note -** gets three beats in any time signature with a 4 as the bottom numeral; equivalent to three quarter notes

18 **Accompaniment -** a part that supports the melody but is subordinate to it

19 **Harmony -** the consonant sounding of two or more notes together

20 **2/4 Time Signature -** two beats in each measure; each quarter note gets one beat.

21 **3/4 Time Signature -** three beats in each measure; each quarter note gets one beat.

22 **Eighth Rest-** gets half a beat in any time signature with a 4 as the bottom numeral

23 **Afterbeat -** a note played on the second half of the beat

24 **Repeat Sign -** means to go back to the beginning of the song or section

25 **Tie -** combines the durations of two notes of the same pitch

26 **First and Second Endings -** play through the first ending, repeat, then skip the first ending and play through the second ending

27 **Round -** music for two or more in which the performers play the same music but start and end at different times

28 **Dotted Quarter Note -** gets one and one half beats in any time signature with a 4 as the bottom numeral; equivalent to three eighth notes

29 **Slur -** a line connecting two or more notes which indicates that only the first note joined by the slur is to be tongued

30 **Pick-up Note/Notes -** the notes in an incomplete measure at the beginning of a song; note values are usually taken from the last measure

31 **Common Time Signature -** the same as 4/4 time

32 **Dynamics -** indicate the relative volume of a note or notes

33 **Key Signature -** sharps or flats placed at the beginning of a section indicating that certain notes are to be sharped or flatted throughout that section

34 **Cut-time -** the same as 2/2 time; two beats in each measure; each half note gets one beat.

35 **Fine -** marks the end of the song

36 **D.C. al Fine -** means to go back to the beginning of the song and play until "Fine" is reached

37 **Syncopation -** an accented note (or stressed note) that comes on an unaccented beat; frequently a note that starts on the up-beat and is held through the next downbeat

38 **Sixteenth Note -** gets one fourth of a beat in any time signature with a 4 as the bottom numeral

39 **6/8 Time Signature -** two beats in each measure; each dotted quarter note gets one beat.

40 **3/8 Time Signature -** one beat in each measure; each dotted quarter note gets one beat.

41 **Fermata -** means to hold the note longer than the indicated value

42 **Flat -** lowers a note one half step

43 **Sharp -** raises a note one half step

44 **Natural -** cancels the effect of a sharp or flat

45 **Repeat Measure -** means to repeat the preceding measure

46 **Double Repeat Measure -** means to repeat the preceding two measures

PUBLICATIONS FOR CLARINET

METHODS
Edited by DAVID HITE

Artistic Studies Bk. 1 from the FRENCH School   B362
40 Studies and 32 Etudes by Cyrill Rose (1830-1903).
All of the classic Rose studies in one volume.

Artistic Studies Bk. 2 from the GERMAN School   B367
Carl Baermann Method: Part IV (selected) and Part V (complete).
Indispensable virtuoso studies for the clarinet.

Artistic Studies Bk. 3 from the ITALIAN School   B390
The best of the Italian operatic-oriented virtuoso studies including the
work of Cavallini, Lebanchi, Magnani, and Gambaro.

Baermann Foundation Studies for Clarinet   B398
An expanded version of the famous Baermann, Part III
method devoted to scales, intervals and chords in all keys.

Melodious and Progressive Studies, Book I   B448
Demnitz: 36 Expressive Studies; Nocentini: 24 Melodic Studies;
Baermann: 24 Melodic Etudes with major and minor scales in thirds.
For study after completion of any beginning clarinet method.

Melodious and Progressive Studies, Book II   B451
Gambaro: 20 Caprices; Dont: 20 Etudes with other special studies.
Valuable as a bridge into the advanced level.

DUETS
Edited by DAVID HITE

Forty Progressive Melodies (Barrett) B382
Seven Grand Concert Duets B521
Includes works by Haydn, Mozart, Crusell and Klose

Three Artistic Duets (Cavallini)   B538
Six Grand Duets (Cavallini)   B539

SOLO REPERTOIRE
with piano accompaniment

LEVEL II
ST790 Minuet and Allegro............................ J.C. BACH-Voxman
SS713 Introduction and Rondo .... DIABELLI-Hite
SS93 Piece in g minor ....Gabriel PIERNE
SU1 Sicilienne ....PARADIS-Hite
SS158 Etude .... RABAUD-Hite
SS76 Wessex Pastorale...................................STOCKS-Bonade

LEVEL III
SS710 Bouree .... BACH-Hite
ST986 Adagio.. BAERMANN -Hite
SS712 Adagio and Gigue ....CORELLI-Hite
ST727 La Fille Au Cheveux de lin .... DEBUSSY -Hite
ST708 Petite Piece .... DEBUSSY -Hite
SS274 Andante de Concert...........................FERLING-JeanJean
SS277 Rigaudon.................................LACOME-Andraud
SS718 Larghetto from Quintet .... MOZART-Hite

LEVEL IV
ST638 Divertimento ....BAERMANN -Forrest
SS717 Andante and Scherzo...DERE-Hite
SS92 Canzonetta....................................Gabriel PIERNE
SS281 Petite Piece ....L. QUET
SS97 Sonata in g minor .... TARTINI-Hite

LEVEL V
ST848 Adagio and Tarantella ....CAVALLINI-Hite
SS276 Fantaisie... Augusta HOLMES
SS282 Solo de Concours...................................... Henri RABAUD
16 Grands Solos de Concert.. D. BONADE

LEVEL VI
ST860 Sonata ....Samuel ADLER
ST909 Intrigues (with band)....................Andreas MAKRIS
ST707 Premiere Rhapsodie................................. DEBUSSY -Hite
ST726 Concerto No.3, Op. 11. .... CRUSELL-Hite

Southern
MUSIC
EXCLUSIVELY DISTRIBUTED BY
HAL•LEONARD

keisersouthernmusic.com